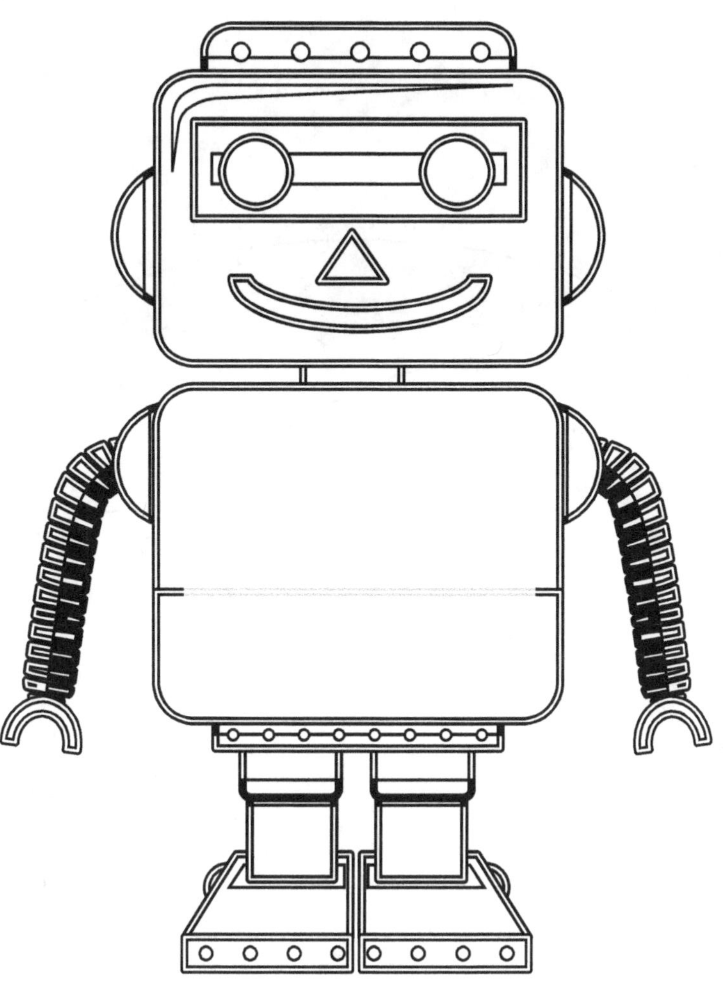

This Belongs To

....

....

....

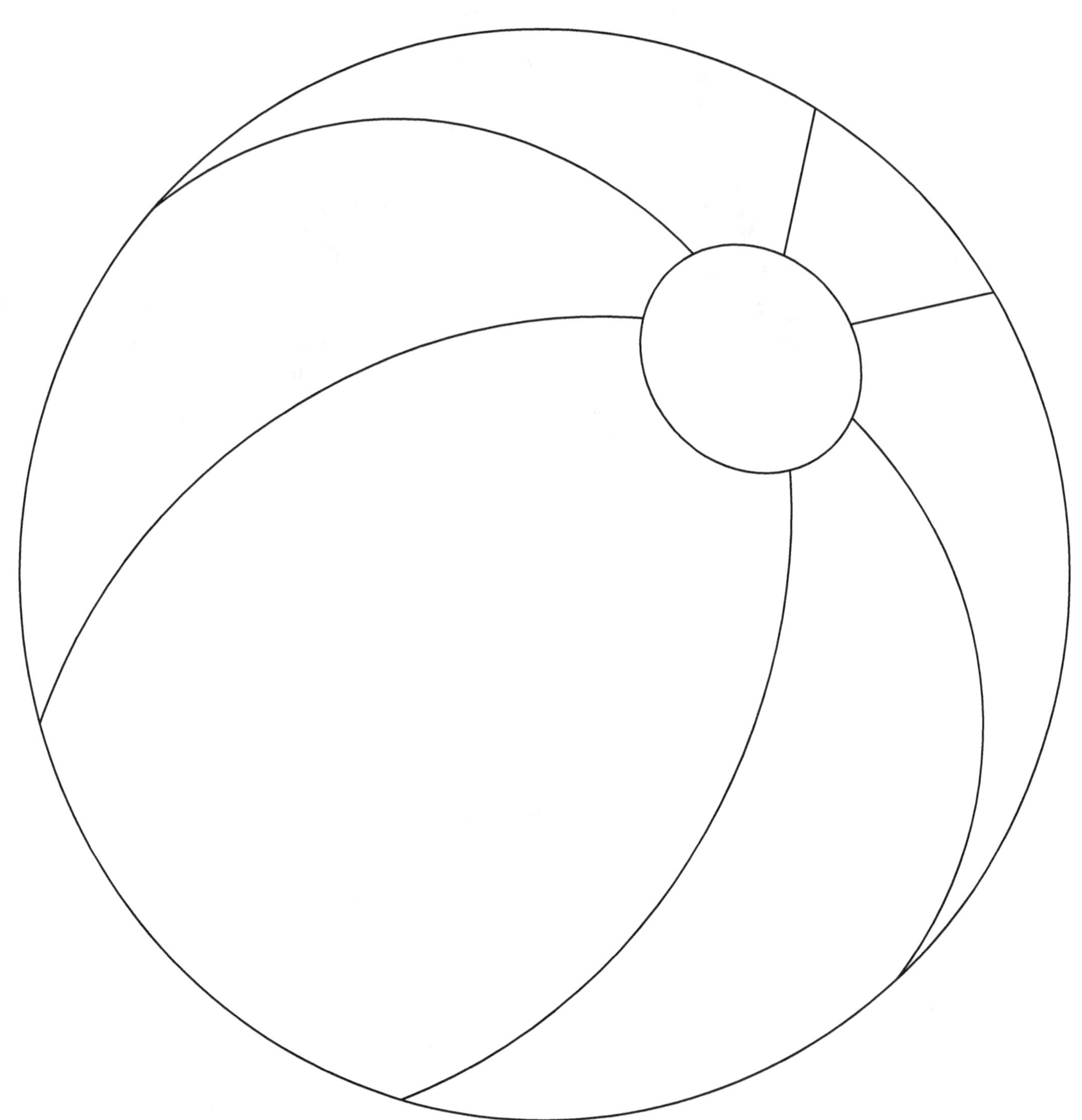

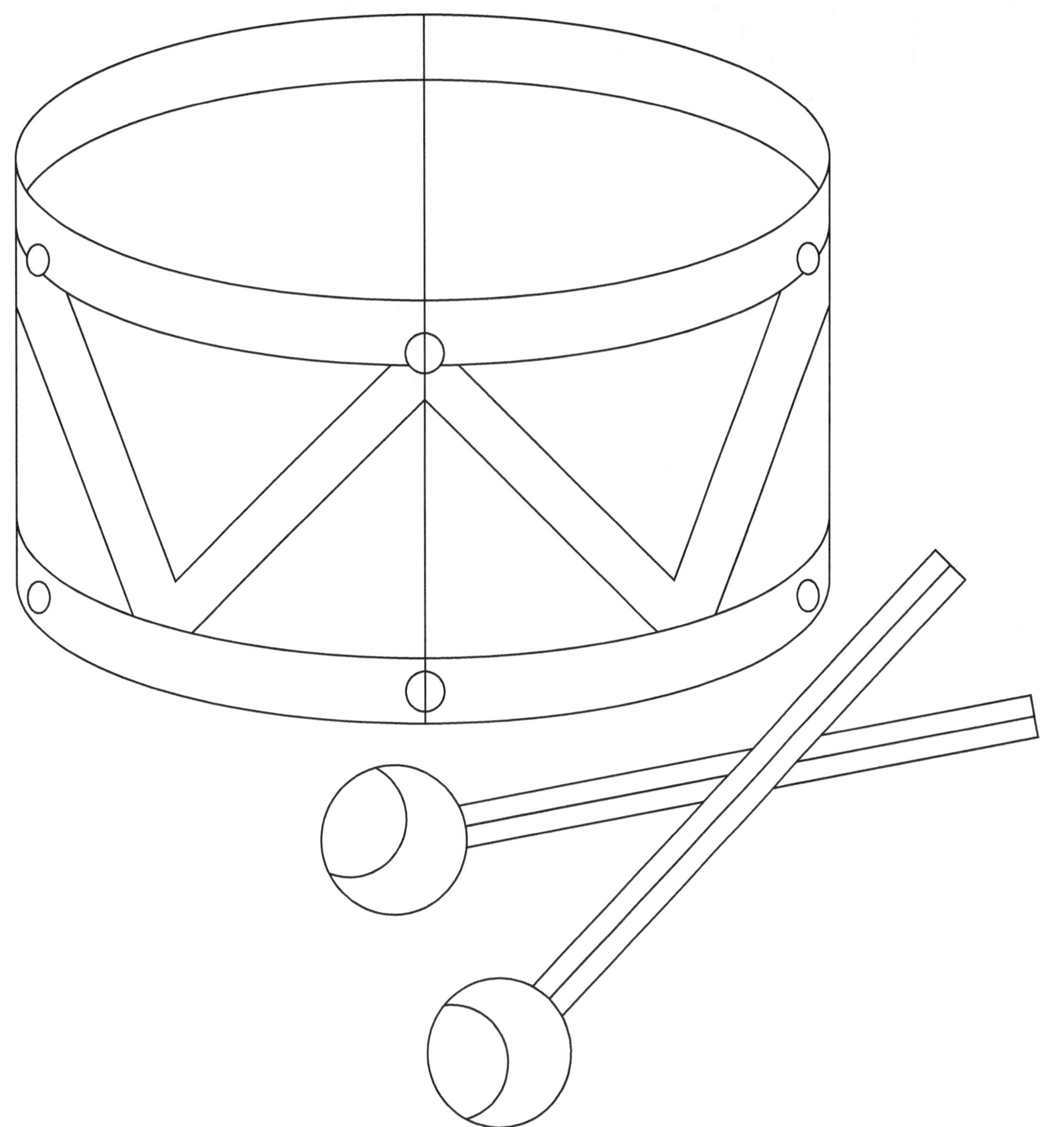

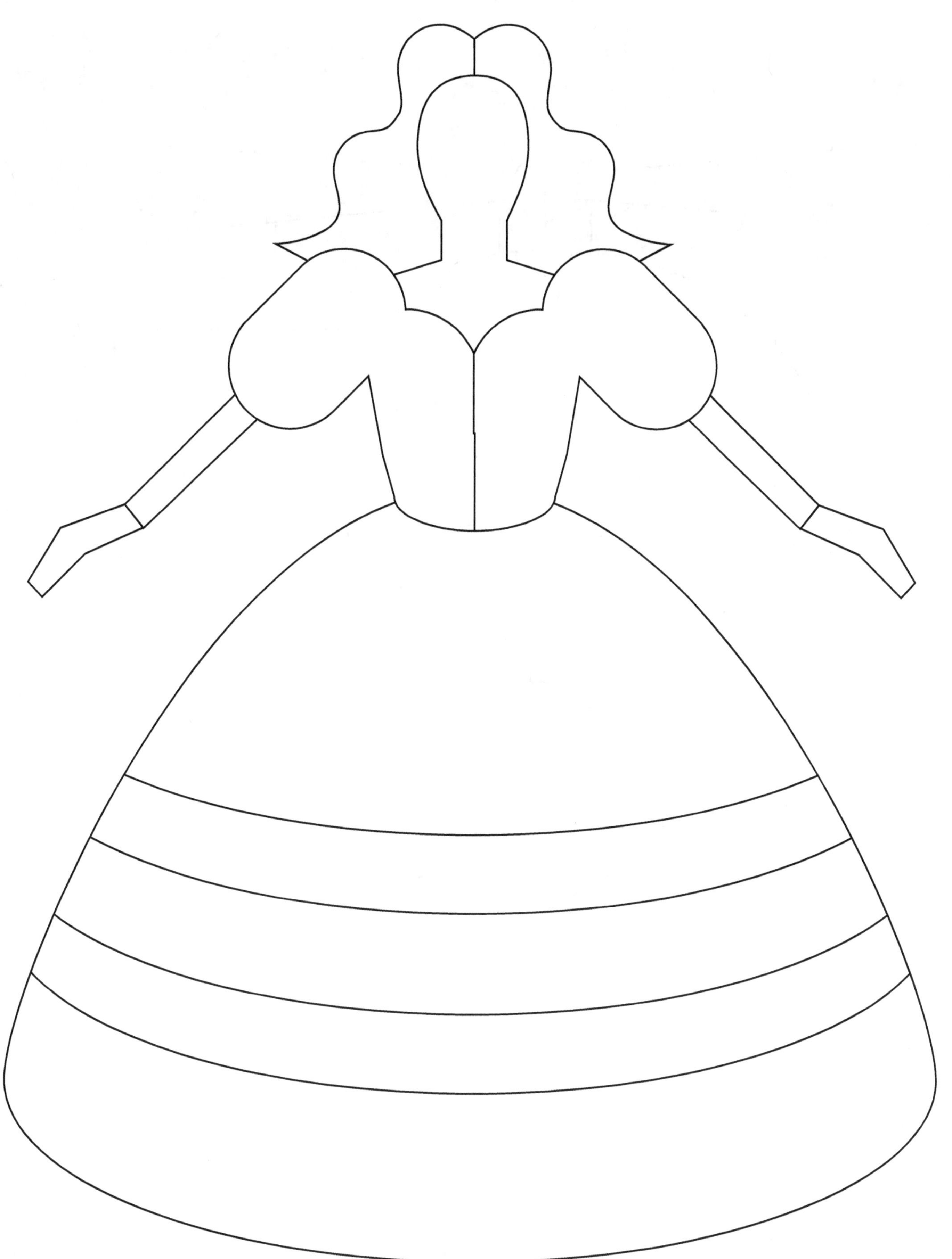

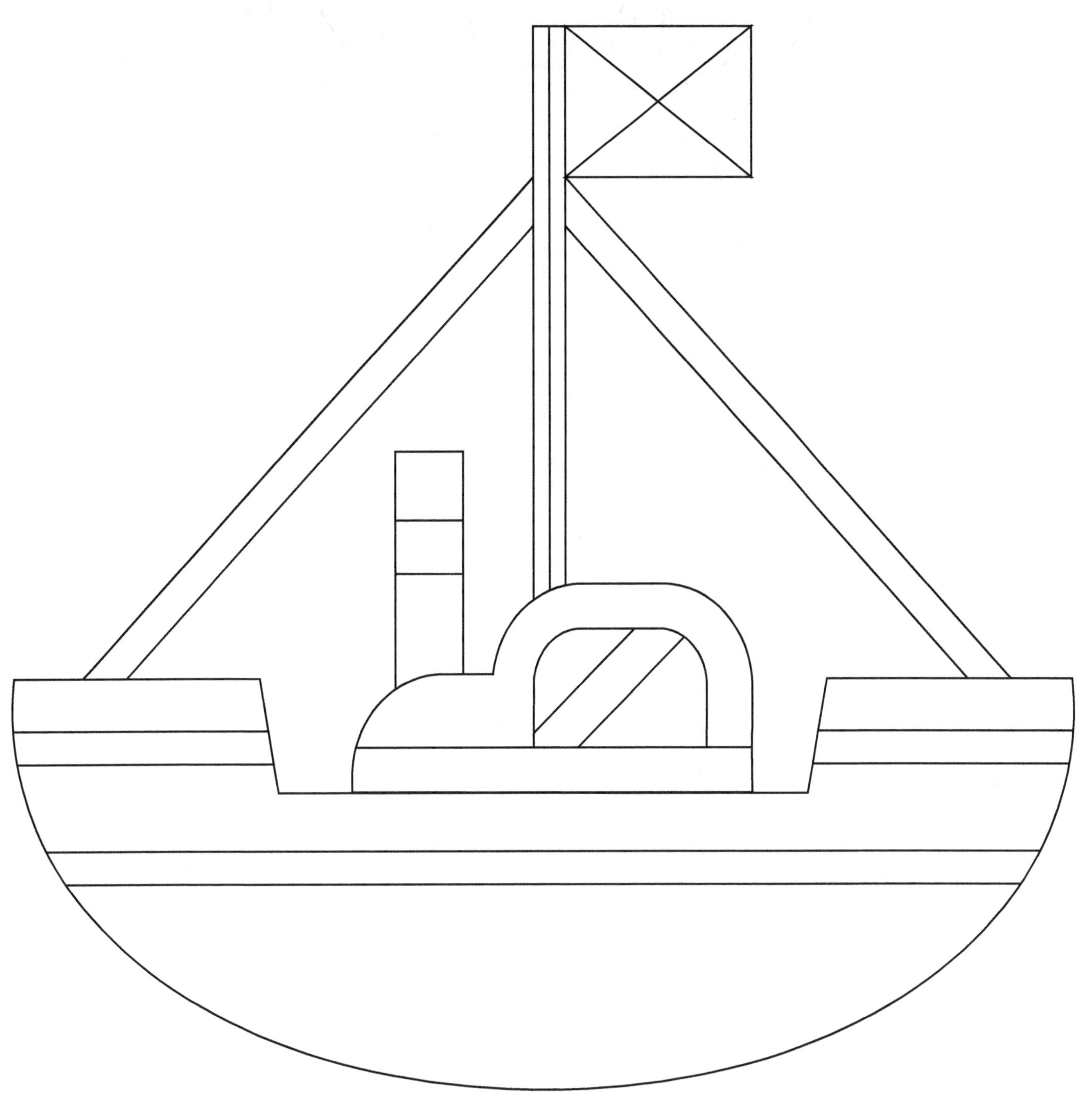

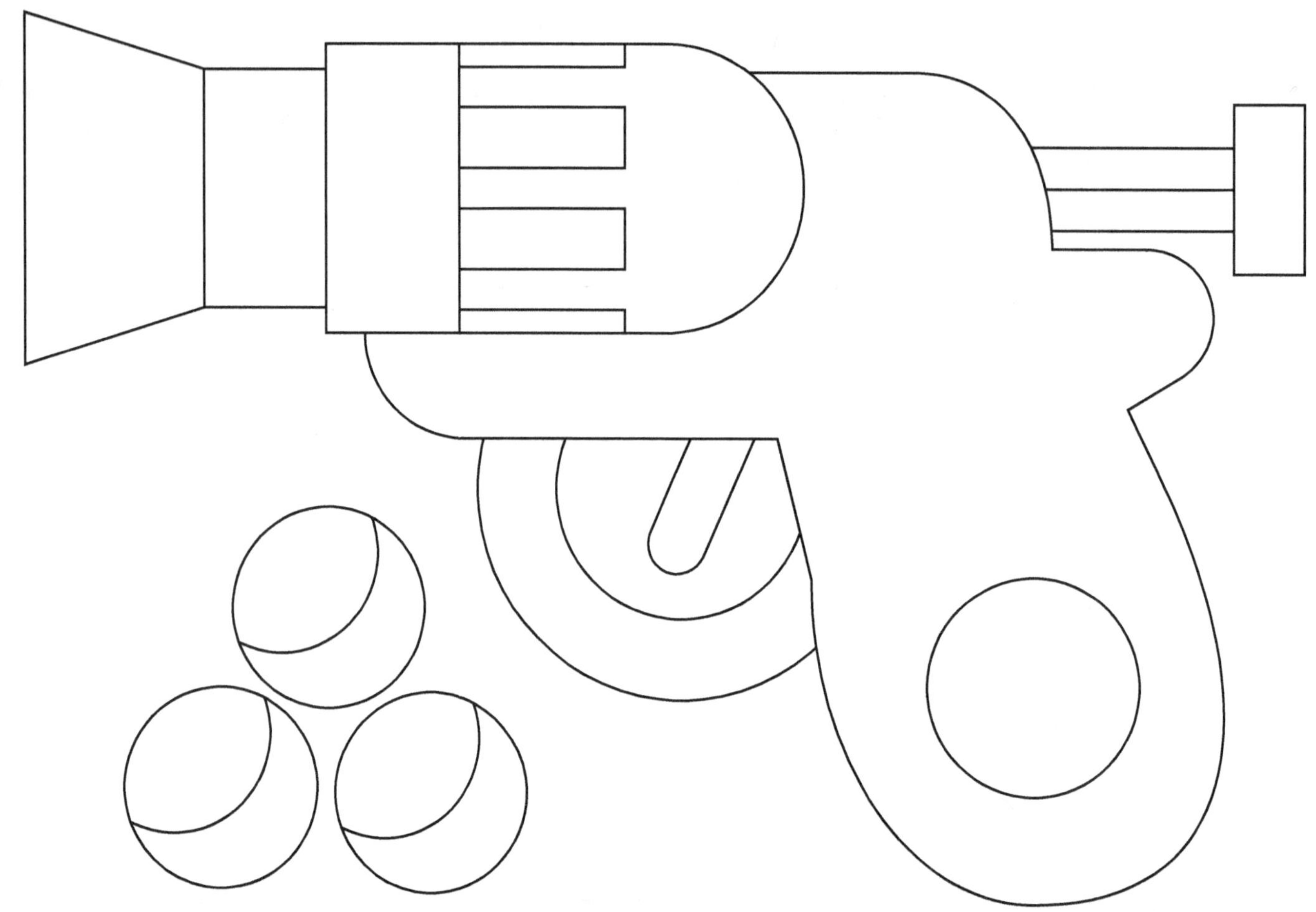

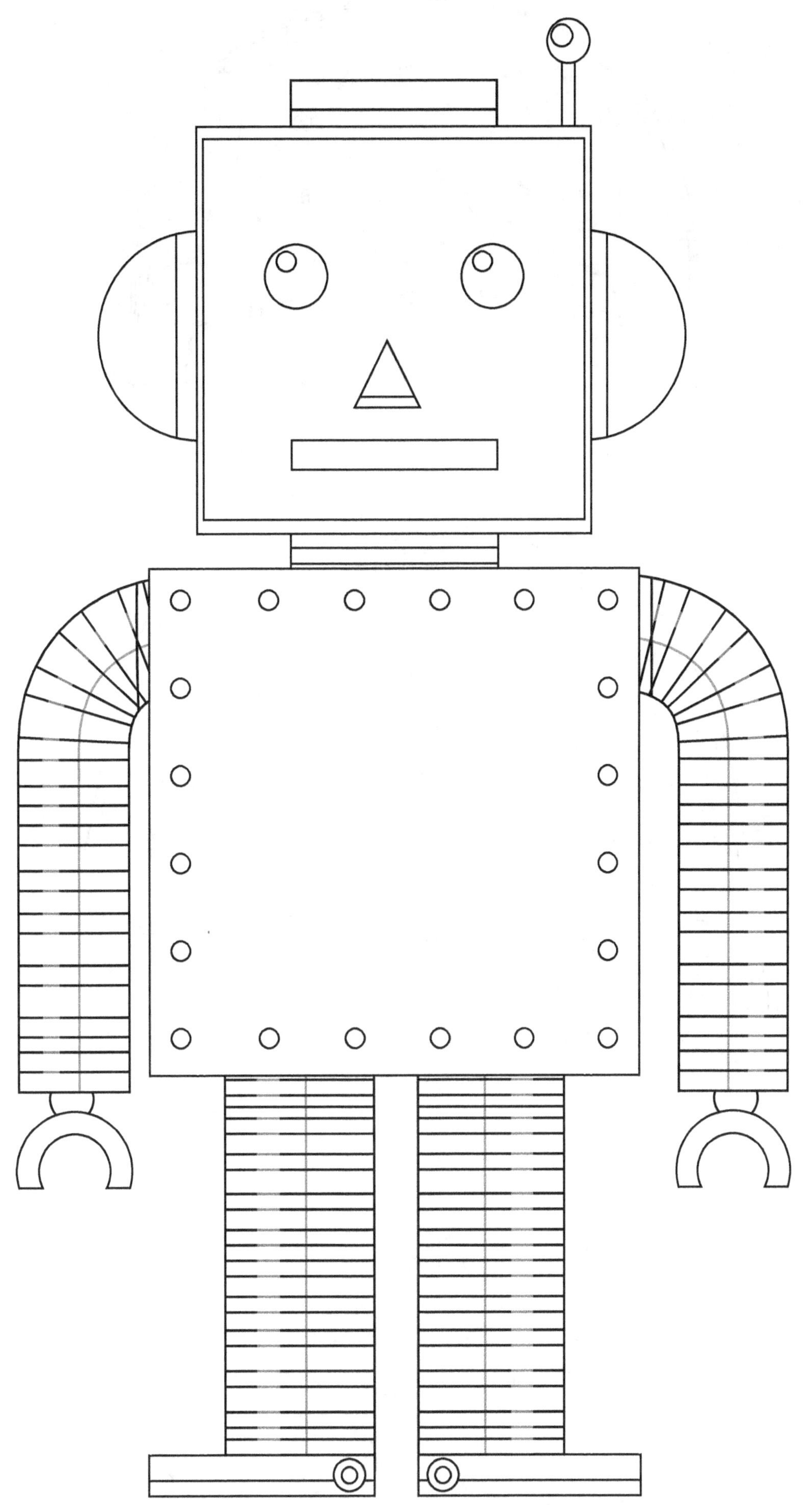

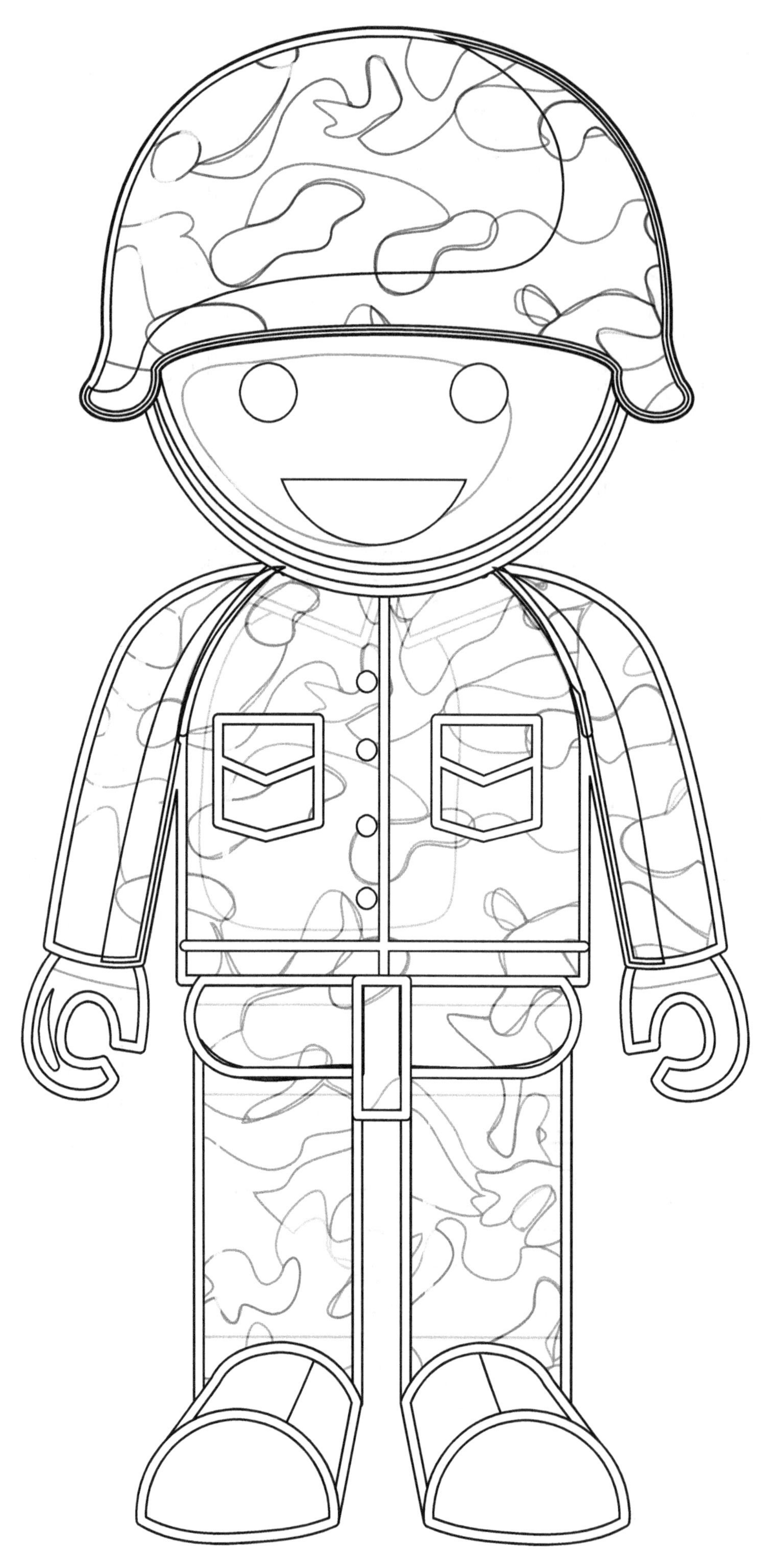

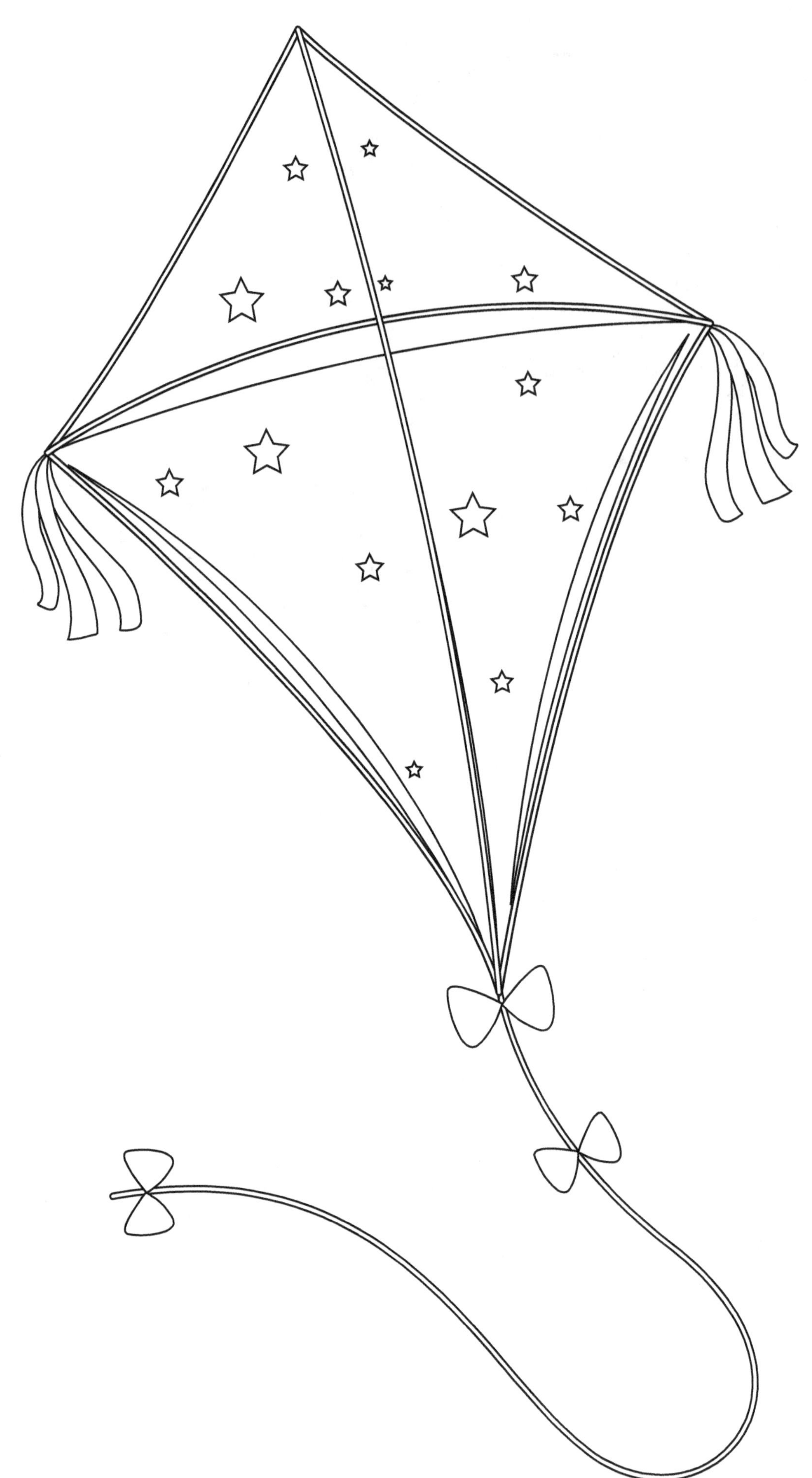

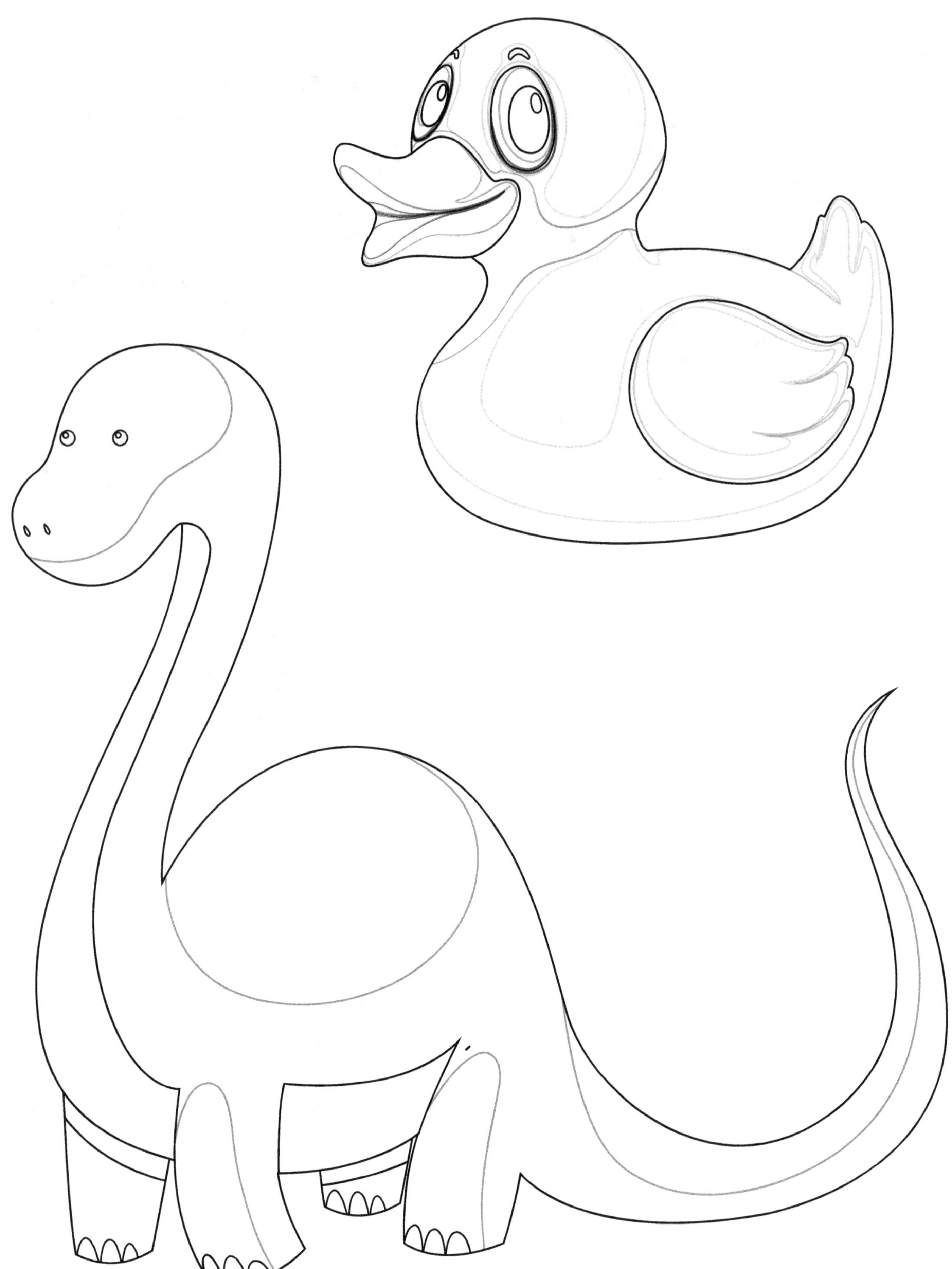

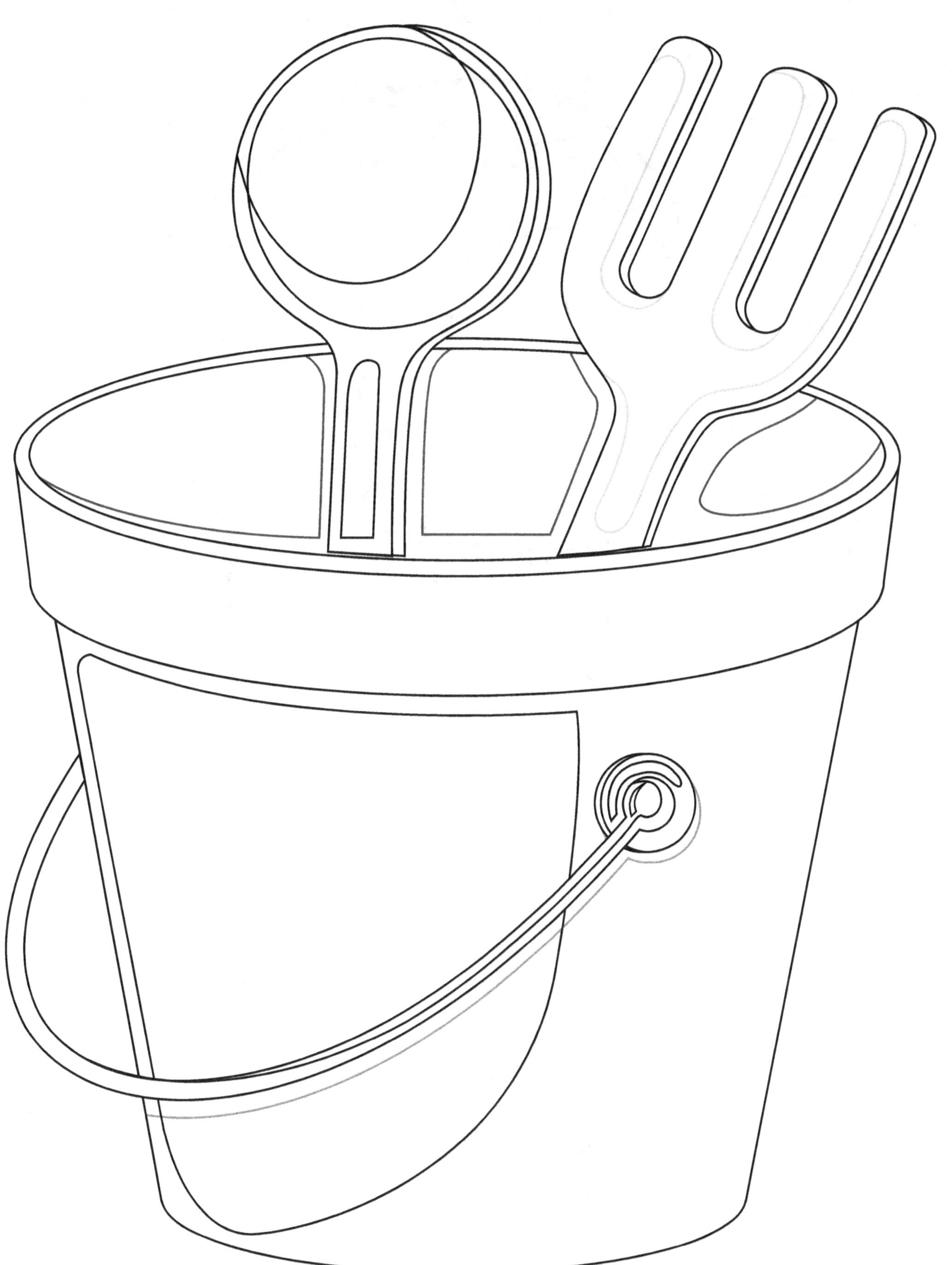